SPARK ISLAND

KS1 National Tests

Reading

Learning Adventures

Contents

Anne Loadman and Sue Richardson

Information for parents

KS1 National Tests

At the end of their final year in KS1, all Year 2 children are assessed on their ability in Reading, Writing (including handwriting), Spelling and Maths. Some of this assessment will be carried out by the class teacher, who will review each child's performance across the whole subject over time, and some of it will take the form of National Tests (popularly knows as SATs).

Tests and teacher assessment are equally important and together they provide a picture of what your child has learned during KS1 and whether he or she is reaching national standards. The school will send you a report at the end of the school year telling you what national curriculum levels your child has reached in the tests and teacher assessment.

Understanding your child's level

There are eight levels in the National Curriculum. On average, children are expected to work their way through one level for every two years they are at school. If your child has achieved the expected level, it means they show knowledge and skills that are the same as, or slightly better than, most children of the same age. By the end of KS1 children should be at Level 2 but there may be some areas they are stronger in and other areas they need more help with. There are some guidelines on page 30 which will help you to work out your child's reading level.

The National Test for English

There are four parts to the English Test:

The reading task

Children working at Level 1 or 2, will complete a reading task. In the task, they will be asked to choose a book to read with their teacher from a suitable selection of children's books. The teacher will also discuss the text with each child. The task assesses accuracy, fluency and understanding.

The reading test

In the reading test, children are given a story and other texts to read and answer questions about. In the Level 2 test, this is contained within one booklet. If your child is judged to be working at Level 3, he or she will receive a story booklet and a separate information text, together with a question booklet to complete. The test assesses your child's ability to read independently and respond in writing to comprehension questions.

The writing test

Your child will be asked to complete two written tasks, one longer and one shorter, which will be carried out on different days.

The spelling test

The spelling test is in two parts. In the first part, the teacher will read out 20 words which your child will write underneath the matching picture. In the second part a piece of text will be read to your child so that he or she can fill in the missing words. Look out for the *Spark Island KS1 National Tests Writing Learning Adventures* activity book which will help your child to prepare for the writing task and spelling test.

About this book

The first part of this book (pages 4-14) provides practice and advice on the different comprehension questions children may be asked. The second section has a practice Level 2 reading test (pages 16-21), together with guidance for assessing your child's level of achievement (page 30). There is also a practice Level 3 reading test (pages 22-29) which you may like to try if he or she has done particularly well with the Level 2 paper (see page 32).

How you can help

You can help your child prepare for the reading task by listening to him or her reading part of an appropriate book aloud. (Some ideas for titles are given at the end of this section.) Encourage your child to read independently wherever possible, but give support where necessary. Then discuss the text together. Some suggestions for questions you could ask are given below. Start with the Level 1 questions and if your child seems to be answering them easily, move on to Level 2.

Level 1

- Which part did you like best?
- Did you find anything funny/sad in the story?
- Who did you like best in the story? Why?
- Who did you not like in the story? Why?
- Did anything surprise you?
- Did you find out anything you did not know before?
- Did you think any of the words were interesting or unusual?
- If this book did not have pictures, would you still like it?

- What do you think will happen next?
- What else would you like to read about in this book?

In the reading task, your child will also have to read a passage aloud to the teacher, who will note down every error he or she makes on a running reading record. This is called a miscue analysis. You can help by listening to your child read *unfamiliar* fiction and non-fiction books and noting down the kind of errors made, and if he or she can correct the error or not. Some children miss words out or are unable to sound some words out phonically. You may be able to help your child learn sounds of which he or she is unsure.

Level 2

Fiction texts

- Do the first few pages of the book make you want to read on? Why?
- How do you think the story is going to end?
- Why do you think this book is called (*title of book*)?
- Which part of the book do you think is the funniest/saddest/most frightening, etc?
- Did the book make you think about anything that has happened to you?
- Do the pictures and the layout of the text help you to understand and enjoy the book better? How do they do this?

Non-fiction texts

- Is this book like a story book?
- What have you found out from reading this book that you did not know before?
- What do you think that page will be about? (*using the page heading as a clue*)
- Does your information book have an index? How would you use it to find something out?
- Do the pictures and the layout of the book make it more interesting and easier to understand? If so, how do they do this?
- Why is that (*heading/word, etc*) written in bold?
- What did you find out about ... ?
- Why do you think that each of the pages has a heading on it?

For all texts, after asking the questions, decide whether your child:

- has understood the main events or ideas in the book
- is able to express preferences and feelings about the book and its characters or subject matter
- has responded to the way the book is written
- is able to give reasons as to why the book was enjoyable.

A guide to assessing your child's reading level is on page 30.

Book suggestions

These books have previously appeared on the National Tests reading list. However as the reading task is supposed to use an unfamiliar text, the books are changed from time to time so children will not become too familiar with them.

Level 1

How do you feel? Gillian Liu and Jane Green, Evans Brothers Ltd, ISBN 0-237-51432-X

Not like that, like this Tony Bradman and Joanna Burroughes, Picture Mammoth, ISBN 0-7497-2415-3

Too much talk Angela Shelf Nedearis, Walker Books Ltd, ISBN 0-7445-4013-5

Frightened Fred Peta Coplens, Andersen Press, ISBN 0-86264-821-1

Level 2

Find out about the body Anita Ganeri, BBC Education, ISBN 0-563-35543-3

Schnitzel von Krumm's Basketwork Lynley Dodd, Picture Puffin, ISBN 0-4-5555-7-9

The Snow Lambs Debi Gliori, Scholastic Ltd, ISBN 0-590-19548-4

The Stars Patrick Moore, Red Fox, ISBN 0-09-967881-0

Tidy up Trevor Rob Lewis, Red Fox, ISBN 0-09-920111-9

Two Little Penguins called Flapjack and Waddle Jacques Duquennoy and Georgie Adams, Orion Children's Books, ISBN 1-85881-110-4

Piska and Pod's adventure

One day, Piska and Pod set off to look for adventure. Piska put some seaweed cakes in a bag in case they got hungry, and Pod took his torch. They were happy because they had found a new cave to explore.

It was very dark in the cave, so Pod put on his torch. Piska could see something at the back of the cave. It looked very big and she was frightened!
'What is it?' she asked.
'I don't know,' said Pod, 'but I'm not going near it! Let's go!'

Tick the right box to answer each question.

1 What is the story about?

☐ a dolphin ☐ Piska and Pod ☐ Sidney the Shark ☐ the beach

2 How were Piska and Pod feeling at the **start** of the story?

☐ excited ☐ sad ☐ happy ☐ frightened

3 What was Pod carrying?

☐ a torch ☐ a bag ☐ a stick ☐ a camera

Piska and Pod tried to run out of the cave.
Then they heard a noise behind them.
They were very scared and Pod dropped his torch.
It was very dark now.
'Don't be scared – it's me!' said a voice from the back of the cave.
'Who are you?' asked Piska, who still couldn't see anything.

'Are you a monster?' asked Pod.
'No, it's me, Norman, the fish who can't swim! I came in here for a rest.'
Piska and Pod were happy to see Norman, and everyone laughed.

Remember
- Read the text carefully.
- Read the questions carefully.
- Don't rush.
- Check your answers.

4 Who was in the cave?

☐ a monster ☐ a shark ☐ Norman ☐ a dolphin

5 What did Pod drop as he ran away?

☐ Piska ☐ his bag ☐ the cakes ☐ his torch

6 What question did Pod ask?

☐ Who is it? ☐ Are you a shark? ☐ Is there anyone there? ☐ Are you a monster?

Water, water!

Water sports

Most people like being near water.

They go to visit: • ponds • rivers • lakes • the sea

Many people enjoy canoeing or rowing on rivers and lakes.

At the seaside, they can go surfing, or ride in motor boats and sailing boats.

Swimming pools make safe places in which to swim. Younger children enjoy paddling pools where the water is not as deep.

Although water can be fun, you should never go near the water without an adult!

1 What do people like doing at the seaside? Write **2** things.

(i) ______________________

(ii) ______________________

2 Why are paddling pools safer than swimming pools for younger children?

____

3 Why do you think you should never go near water without an adult?

____

____

Tiny creatures

Piska and Pod like reading about other lands.

This table is about insects and their habits.

Insect	**Lives ...**	**Eats ...**	**Is it harmful?**
Housefly 	*In houses and other warm places*	*Tiny pieces of food*	*Spreads germs*
Furniture beetle 	*In wooden furniture and the beams of houses*	*Tiny pieces of wood*	*Can make roofs collapse and damage furniture*
Flea 	*On animals, such as cats and dogs*	*Bites animals and eats tiny amounts of their blood*	*Can cause itching and spots where it bites*

1 What does each insect eat? Match the boxes.

flea

furniture beetle

housefly

blood

food

wood

2 Why can a housefly be harmful? ____________________

3 Which insect might you find in a wooden chair? ____________________

4 Where would be a good place for a flea to live?

____

5 Which insect do you think is the most dangerous in the table? Why?

____

____

Trapped!

On a ledge in a deep pool in Sparklantis, there sat a large Clamp, with its jaws shut.

Now everyone knew that, when you swam past a Clamp, its mouth would open and you would see its long tongue holding exactly what you most wanted in the world. However, everyone also knew that if you tried to grab it, the Clamp would quickly snap its jaws shut! You would be trapped! To escape, the Clamp would make you solve a riddle – and the Clamp's riddles were very tricky.

One day, when Maurice and Melvin Mullet were out for a swim, Maurice spotted a Clamp. 'I wonder what that Clamp is hiding in its mouth?' he said to Melvin. 'I hope it's a nice cake!'
'Well, I hope it's a new hairbrush – mine's so old now,' said Melvin.

1 Why do you think the Clamps hold treasure in their mouth?

I think that the Clamps hold treasure in their mouth so that anyone who passes would stop and try to take it. Then the Clamps could trap them until they answer a riddle.

2 Why do you think the Clamps have jaws that could snap shut fast?

____

____

3 What do you think will happen to Maurice and Melvin Mullet?

____

____

Maurice swam up to the Clamp, which promptly stuck out its tongue. There, on the very end of its tongue, sat the most delicious chocolate cake that Maurice had ever seen!

'I must have it!' thought Maurice. He was just about to take a bite when the Clamp's mouth snapped shut. 'Now you'll have to solve a riddle!' said Melvin.

This is what the Clamp asked:

> 'I have a mouth but cannot speak.
> I have two banks but no money.
> What am I?'

Maurice thought and thought. In the end, he got the right answer. Can you?

4 Why do you think the Clamp put the cake right on the end of its tongue?

5 What do you think would have been on the Clamp's tongue if he wanted to trap Melvin? Why do you think this?

6 If you were Melvin, what would you have said to Maurice when he went up to the Clamp? Why?

Answer to the riddle: a river

Pod's poem

Darting like a silver streak
Flashing through the reeds.
The minnow swims the river
Looking for a feed.

Children on the riverbank
Are fishing with their nets.
Swim fast, little minnow,
They haven't caught you yet!

Remember

Whatever the text type, the rules are the same:

- Read the text carefully.
- Read the questions carefully.
- Think before writing your answer.
- Read the text again if you need to.

1 What kind of fish is mentioned in the poem? ______

2 What are the children trying to do? ______

3 What colour is the minnow? ______

4 Which **2** words in the poem show that the minnow is moving quickly?

______ ______

5 How do you think the minnow is feeling? Tick **2** boxes.

☐ happy ☐ frightened ☐ excited ☐ worried

6 Choose the best title for the poem. Tick **1** box.

☐ Children fishing ☐ A silver streak

☐ The jolly fish ☐ On the riverbank

A letter from King Porus

Look at important things like the address,

The Royal Palace
1 Atlantean Way
Sparklantis

14 February — the date,

Dear Prince Pomona, — and who the letter is for.

We would like to invite you and your family to join us for the celebration of Piska and Pod's birthday. We are planning a big party with food and dancing on Saturday, 7th June, at 2 o'clock, in the palace.

Please let me know if you can come.

Your friend,

King Porus of Sparklantis

1 **Who** wrote the letter?

____

2 **What** are they celebrating?

____

3 **When** is the party?

____

4 **Where** will it take place?

____

Melvin's mobile

How to make a fish mobile

What you need

- thick thread

- glue stick

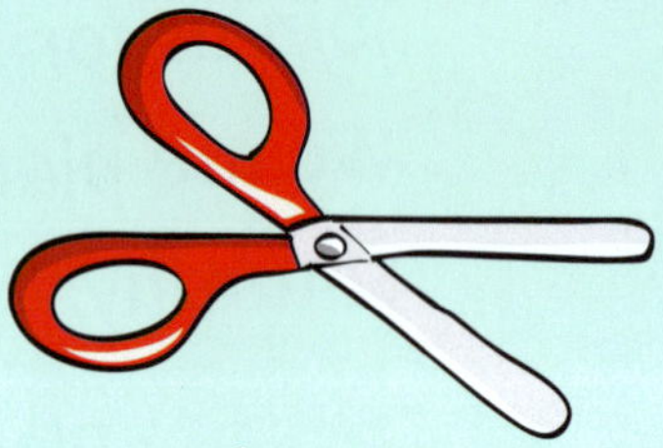

- scissors

- a pencil

- pieces of card – white or coloured

- tin foil, sweet wrappers or wrapping paper

- two buttons or sequins

- sticky tape

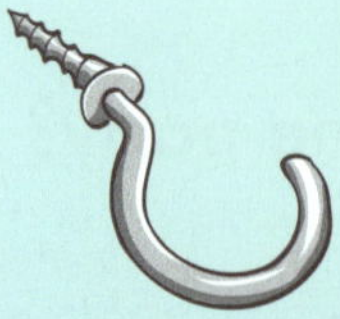

- a cup hook

1 Do you need these things?
Put a ✓ or a ✗ in each box.

	✓ or ✗
felt tipped pen	
pencil	
glue	
scissors	

2 What kind of thread do you need?

____

3 Why do you think the instructions tell you what you need first, before telling you what to do?

____

____

____

Now turn over to find out how to make your mobile!

Copy this fish shape onto card.

What to do

1 Take your card and cut it into a fish shape.

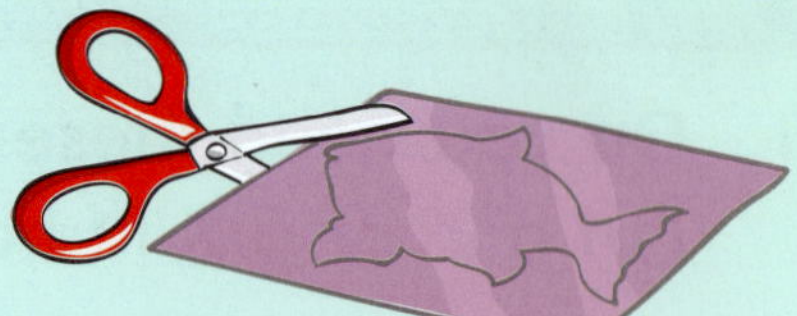

2 Cut out pieces of tin foil and sweet wrappers to make scales.

3 Put glue onto the card fish and stick the scales all over your fish. Make sure you don't leave any card showing.

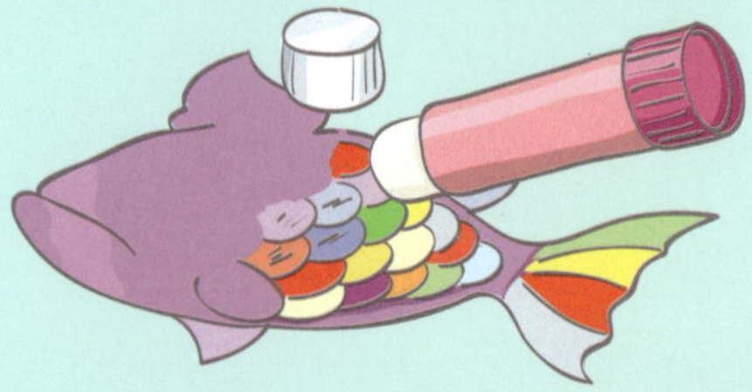

4 When the glue is dry, turn the fish over and stick scales on the other side.

5 Stick a button or sequin for an eye on each side of the fish.

6 Ask an adult to stick the thread onto the fish, then you can hang it from the ceiling or in a window, using the hook.

You could make lots of fish and put them on threads of different lengths to make a big fish mobile. When there's a breeze, your fish will look as if they are swimming!

4 What can you use to make the fish's eye? ______

5 What do you use the sweet wrappers for?

______

6 Why do you have to wait for the glue to dry before turning the fish over?

______

7 Why do you need to put string or thread onto the fish?

______

KS1 Reading practice tests

The seashell surprise

LEVEL 2

One sunny day, Joe and his sister Leanne went out in the car with their Mum and Dad. They had no idea where they were going and they were very excited. At last, the car stopped.
'Hooray, we're at the beach!' shouted Joe.
'Let's go and splash in the water!' said Leanne.
Mum said, 'I think we should find a good place to sit first.'

The beach was full of people. The sun was hot and boys and girls were playing in the sea. Some children were digging holes for the sea to fill with water. Some children were making sandcastles.
'Come on,' said Joe. 'Let's go and swim.'
'Good idea,' said Mum. 'Dad will go with you.'

1 Who did Joe and Leanne go to the beach with?

☐ Mum ☐ Dad

☐ on their own ☐ Mum and Dad

1 — 1 mark

2 Finish these sentences. Join the boxes.

The beach was	excited.
The sun was	crowded.
Joe and Leanne were	shining.
The holes were	full of water.

2 — 1 mark

3 What did Leanne want to do when she got to the beach?

____

3 — 1 mark

4 Who would look after Joe and Leanne in the water? ____________

4 — 1 mark

The two children ran to the sea and played in the water. They splashed and swam and jumped over the waves, until Dad said it was time for lunch.

Joe and Leanne had sandwiches, crisps, juice and an apple. They wanted to go back in the sea but Mum said, 'Let's look on the sand first and see what we can find.'

The sea had washed in lots of things for them to find. They saw wood and stones and they picked up shells and put them in their bucket. Then they went back to make a sandcastle. 'We can put the shells on the sandcastle,' said Leanne.

5 Write down **2** things the children had to eat.

______________________ ______________________

5 — **1** mark

6 Write down **2** things the children saw on the beach.

______________________ ______________________

6 — **1** mark

7 What did the children put in the bucket?

____

7 — **1** mark

8 What were the children going to make?

____

8 — **1** mark

As they were digging, Joe noticed that the bucket was moving on its own!
'Hey!' he shouted. 'Look, Leanne, the bucket is MAGIC!'

They shouted for Mum. She picked up the bucket and looked inside. 'See,' she said. 'One of your shells had a crab in it. The crab lives inside the shell, but it hides if anyone comes near it. We must have scared it.'
Everyone laughed.
'We'd better put it back in the sea,' said Mum.

9 — 1 mark

9 Why is the word 'MAGIC' written in capital letters?

- ☐ to show it is a new word
- ☐ to show that Joe is shouting
- ☐ to show Joe is whispering
- ☐ to show it is a magic word

10 — 1 mark

10 Why was the bucket moving?

- ☐ It was magic.
- ☐ The sea moved it.
- ☐ A crab was inside.
- ☐ Leanne moved it.

11 — 1 mark

11 Find a word in the story that means the same as **frightened**. ____________________

12 — 1 mark

12 How do you think Joe and Leanne were feeling at the end of the story?

- ☐ sad
- ☐ frightened
- ☐ tired
- ☐ happy

Boats

LEVEL 2

1 How does a canoe move through the water? 1

_______________________________________ 1 mark

2 How do some boats use the wind to help them move along? 2

____

_______________________________________ 1 mark

3 What kind of boat would you use to explore the seabed? 3

_______________________________________ 1 mark

The seashore

LEVEL 2

The salty sea
Most of the Earth is covered by sea. Sea water is salty. The seashore is where the land and the sea meet. It can be sandy or rocky.

Rock pools
Rock pools are formed when the tide goes out and some sea water is left trapped in the rocks. Small sea creatures live in the rock pools.

Shell dwellers
Hermit crabs live in the shells of other animals that have died. When they grow too big for the shell, they 'move house' by finding a larger shell.

1 The writing 'The seashore' is:

- [ ] a poem
- [ ] a set of facts
- [ ] a story
- [ ] a play

1 — 1 mark

2 When are rock pools formed?

____

2 — 1 mark

3 What happens when a hermit crab gets too big for its shell?

____

____

3 — 1 mark

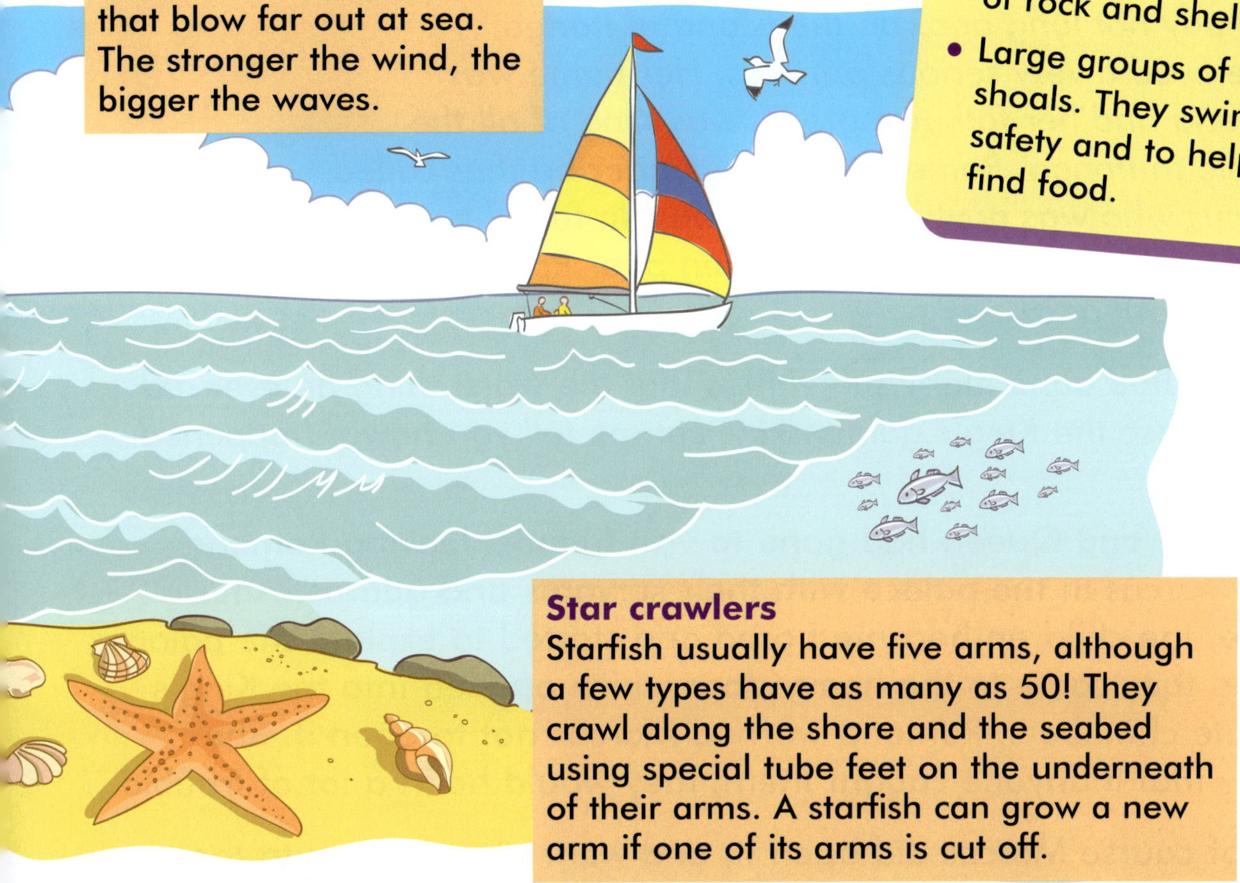

Wind and waves
Waves are made by winds that blow far out at sea. The stronger the wind, the bigger the waves.

Did you know?

- Sand is made from tiny pieces of rock and shells.
- Large groups of fish are called shoals. They swim together for safety and to help each other find food.

Star crawlers
Starfish usually have five arms, although a few types have as many as 50! They crawl along the shore and the seabed using special tube feet on the underneath of their arms. A starfish can grow a new arm if one of its arms is cut off.

4 What are large groups of fish called? ______________________ 4 1 mark

5 Why do some fish swim in shoals? Tick **2** boxes. 5 1 mark

☐ because they are lonely ☐ in case they get lost

☐ to help each other find food ☐ to keep safe

6 How do starfish move? 6 1 mark

____

____

7 How are waves made? 7 1 mark

____

____

LEVEL 3

The magic key

One day not long ago, on the island of Itonga, there lived a very serious princess. Her name was Romena and her father, Agreus, was King of all the people in Itonga. Romena had a younger brother called Marcus who was anything but serious. In fact, he was always getting into trouble and then poor Romena had to get him out of it!

Marcus had done many silly things, but the worst thing he ever did was to lose the King's golden key. Let me tell you how it happened.

The King and Queen had gone to visit friends, leaving Romena and Marcus in the palace with their servants and guards. After a while, the children became bored and started to explore the palace. When they came to the heavy door which opened into the King's private chambers, Romena warned Marcus not to open it. She knew that if anyone caught them, they would be in a lot of trouble.

But of course Marcus did open it, and went straight over to the King's desk. There, he saw a large, golden key. 'I wonder what this opens,' he said to himself. 'Put it back now!' shouted Romena.

1 What was the name of Marcus's sister?

____

1 — 1 mark

2 On which island did Romena and her brother live?

____

2 — 1 mark

3 Explain how the golden key fell out of the window.

____

____

3 — 1 mark

4 Who or what swallowed the golden key?

☐ a fish ☐ a bird ☐ a servant ☐ a fox

4 — 1 mark

She tried to grab the key from Marcus, but it slipped out of his hand and flew through an open window. There it lay, shining on the sand below them.

'Quick!,' said Romena. 'Let's get it back!' But before they could get to the key, they saw a big black and white bird fly up and swallow it whole! 'Now what are we going to do?' asked Romena. 'I don't know,' said Marcus, 'but we'll have to hurry. Mum and Dad will be home soon.'

So they went to see the wise turtle who lived in a small cave near the palace. He popped his wise head out of his shell and listened to their problem. Then the turtle nodded his head slowly and said, 'The key you describe is very important. It is the key that controls the tides around Itonga. It must be turned twice a day or else the island will flood because the tide will not go out. The whole island will be ruined if you don't get the key back quickly. The tide is due to turn in one hour. You don't have much time!'

5 Why do you think the children went to the turtle for advice?

____

5

1 mark

6 How do you think Romena and Marcus felt when the key fell out of the window?

____

____

6

1 mark

7 Why was the golden key so important? What did it do?

____

____

____

7

1 mark

The turtle whispered a plan to the children and they set off immediately. The turtle had recognised the bird who had eaten the key and knew where it lived.

Romena explained to the bird what had happened and luckily the bird wanted to help them.

'The turtle said you might be able to sneeze the key out,' said Marcus. 'I must admit it's a good idea,' said the bird, 'but I don't feel very sneezy at the moment.'

8 How did Rowena make the bird sneeze?

8 — 1 mark

9 How do you think Rowena and Marcus felt when they got the key back? Tick 2 boxes.

- [ ] relieved
- [ ] excited
- [ ] worried
- [ ] happy

9 — 1 mark

10 How did the king's carriage move along?

10 — 1 mark

Gently, Romena tickled the bird's nose with her pony tail and, before long, the bird let out the most enormous sneeze.

The golden key shot out onto the sand. 'Hooray!' shouted Marcus. 'Thank you ***so*** much,' said Romena. 'Now let's get this key back where it belongs.'

The children put the key back on the desk just as the King's carriage arrived, pulled by two golden horses. 'Hello, dears,' said the King. 'Had a good day?'

'Oh, nothing much happened,' said Romena. 'Nothing exciting at all!' And she looked at Marcus, who had gone bright red, and smiled.

11 Why do you think Marcus went red when his father asked if they had had a good day? 11

____

____

1 mark

12 Find the best word to describe the golden key. 12
It was ...

☐ important ☐ interesting

☐ enormous ☐ complicated

1 mark

LEVEL 3

Seaside towns

There is more to a seaside town than buckets and spades and a trip to the pier. It is also a place where people live and work.

Scarborough

There are many seaside towns in Britain. Some are small, like Bude in Cornwall, and some are large, like Blackpool and Scarborough. Many of the oldest towns used to be fishing ports.

A lot of seaside towns are popular because they have sandy beaches and sheltered bays, which makes them good places to take a holiday.

1 Find and copy the names of 2 seaside towns in the text.

______________________ ______________________

1 — 1 mark

2 How did most seaside towns start?

- [ ] as holiday resorts
- [ ] as fishing ports
- [ ] as big towns
- [ ] as piers

2 — 1 mark

3 Which of these are you most likely to find on a pier?

- [ ] shells
- [ ] a swimming pool
- [ ] amusement arcades
- [ ] a lighthouse

3 — 1 mark

4 How are many lighthouses operated these days?

____

4 — 1 mark

Some seaside towns have a lighthouse or a pier, which are good fun to visit. Many lighthouses are operated by computers now, but in the past people used to live in them. Their job was to warn sailors of dangerous rocks by shining a big light out over the sea.

It is exciting to go to the top of a lighthouse, or to walk along a wooden pier and see the sea far beneath your feet. Some piers have a fair, amusement arcades and stalls selling sweets and drinks on them. Blackpool has three piers!

In Britain, the weather is not always fine and sunny, so it is important that seaside towns have places where people can go when the weather is bad. On this map of Scarborough, you can see things to do when the weather is sunny, but there is also a lot to do if it rains.

5 Why do we need lighthouses?

5 **1 mark**

6 Why is it important for seaside towns in Britain to have things for people to do inside as well as outside?

6 **1 mark**

7 Look at the map of Scarborough and write down something you might do if the weather was rainy.

7 **1 mark**

8 Why do you think seaside towns make good places for a holiday?

8 **1 mark**

LEVEL 3

By the sea

Children laughing,
Waves crashing,
Crabs in rocks,
Sand in socks.

Fairground rides,
Swings and slides,
Hook the duck,
Try your luck.

Boating trips,
Fish and chips.
Jump the waves,
Explore caves.

Sunny skies,
Buzzing flies.
Seagulls glide,
While wise fish hide.

Shells to pick,
Cones to lick.
I love to be,
by the sea!

1 How do you know that the children in the poem were happy?

____

1 — 1 mark

2 From the poem, find 2 things you could do at the fairground.

_______________ _______________

2 — 1 mark

3 From the third verse of the poem, find a word which means the same as to 'investigate'.

____

3 — 1 mark

4 How does the writer of the poem feel about being by the seaside?

____

____

____

____

4 — 1 mark

5 Write down two pairs of rhyming words to be found in the poem.

_______________ and _______________

_______________ and _______________

6 What is the weather like in the poem?

____

7 In verse 4 why do you think the fish are hiding?

____

____

8 What kind of noise do the flies make in the poem?

____

9 Which verb describes the way the seagulls are moving?

____

10 If you were at the beach in the poem, which of the activities would you like to do?

____

____

____

____

____

____

____

____

____

5 1 mark

6 1 mark

7 1 mark

8 1 mark

9 1 mark

10 1 mark

Assessing your child's reading level

The following statements should help you to estimate the level at which your child is reading. Read all the statements for a particular level and see in which level your child 'best fits'.

Level 1

- [ ] Recognizes familiar words from a simple text
- [ ] When reading aloud, uses knowledge of letters, sounds and symbols to read words and establish meaning
- [ ] Sometimes needs support for the above activities
- [ ] Prompted by questions, replies by identifying parts he or she liked or found interesting

Level 2C

- [ ] Reads more than 90% of a text independently
- [ ] Most of reading was accurate
- [ ] Uses appropriate strategies (starting to sound out familiar sight words)
- [ ] Reads from word to word
- [ ] Pauses to talk about text and confirm meaning
- [ ] Can comment on obvious characteristics (e.g. good/bad characters)
- [ ] Can retell a story, but retell will either be too short or too long and will rely heavily on any illustrations

Level 2B

- [ ] Reading is almost entirely accurate
- [ ] Sometimes notices when reading doesn't make sense (by self-correcting or attempting to resolve a problem, even if the strategy used is unhelpful)
- [ ] Is able to read ahead
- [ ] Well paced in parts, taking account of punctuation
- [ ] Comments on setting
- [ ] Comments on how plot links together and contains surprises
- [ ] Can make reference to the way in which a book is set out (presentation)
- [ ] When retelling, refers to most of the main characters and events
- [ ] Relies mainly on remembering shared text rather than on passage read alone

Level 2A

- [ ] Reading is accurate
- [ ] Notices when reading does not make sense and takes action (self-corrects; looks back/forwards in text; asks for meaning)
- [ ] Tackles unfamiliar words with encouragement only
- [ ] Is able to read ahead and uses expression and intonation to enhance meaning
- [ ] Pace and fluency of independent reading shows confidence
- [ ] Can identify and comment on the main characters and how they relate to one another
- [ ] Can respond to questions about alternatives or extensions to events and actions
- [ ] Can comment about feelings created by the story
- [ ] Re-telling is clear and balanced
- [ ] Is able to comment about some of the ways in which the book is written and presented

Level 3

- [ ] Reading is accurate with few errors (of a Level 3 text)
- [ ] Can read a range of texts with increasing fluency
- [ ] Reading is at an independent level. Needing little support
- [ ] Uses a variety of appropriate strategies to establish meaning
- [ ] Shows understanding of main points of both fiction and non-fiction texts
- [ ] Can express preferences
- [ ] Uses knowledge of the alphabet to locate books and finds information using an index

Answers

Pages 4-5 Piska and Pod's adventure

1 Piska and Pod
2 happy
3 a torch
4 Norman
5 his torch
6 Are you a monster?

Page 6 Water, water!

1 surfing, riding in motor boats or sailing boats
2 The water is not as deep.
3 *Accept any answer like*: the adult keeps you safe; it is dangerous to go near water by yourself; you might drown; you might get into trouble, etc.

Page 7 Tiny creatures

1 furniture beetle – wood; flea – blood; housefly – food
2 It spreads germs.
3 A furniture beetle
4 On animals like cats and dogs
5 *Accept any insect as long as the reason matches the choice, e.g.* I think the flea is the most dangerous because it bites your blood and makes you itch.

Pages 8-9 Trapped!

Answers to these questions are the children's opinions and thoughts, so a definitive answer is hard to make. These are suggestions only. Accept any reasonable answer.

2 The Clamps could shut their jaws fast to trap people so that they can't get away.
3 I think Maurice or Melvin will get trapped by the Clamp.
4 I think the Clamp put the cake on the end of it's tongue to make Maurice try to grab it.
5 I think there would have been a new hairbrush on the Clamp's tongue, because Melvin wanted a new one so much.
6 I would have said, 'Don't go near the Clamp, Maurice – you'll get trapped.'

Page 10 Pod's poem

1 a minnow
2 catch fish
3 silver
4 darting; flashing
5 frightened; worried
6 *Your child's choice from the selection given. Only one box should be ticked.*

Page 11 A letter from King Porus

1 King Porus (of Sparklantis)
2 Piska and Pod's birthday
3 Saturday 7th June at 2 o'clock
4 at the palace

Pages 12-14 Melvin's mobile

1

	✓ or ✗
felt tipped pen	✗
pencil	✓
glue	✓
scissors	✓

2 thick
3 so that you will know what you need to get before you start making it; in case you forget anything (*or similar*)
4 sequins or buttons
5 to make scales
6 so the scales on the first side don't fall off (*or similar*)
7 to hang it up

Practice reading tests

Pages 16-18 The seashell surprise

1 Mum and Dad
2 The beach was crowded; The sun was shining; Joe and Leanne were excited; The holes were full of water.
3 Leanne wanted to splash in the water.
4 Dad
5 *Two from:* sandwiches, crisps, juice, apple
6 *Two from:* wood, stones, shells
7 shells
8 a sandcastle
9 to show that Joe is shouting
10 A crab was inside.
11 scared
12 happy *or* tired

Page 19 Boats

1 You have to paddle it; You use a paddle/oars (*children may put oars, as it is in the text - in this case 'oars' is acceptable*)
2 They have sails to catch the wind. The wind blows them along.
3 a submarine

Page 20-21 The seashore

1 a set of facts
2 when the tide goes out and sea water is trapped in the rocks
3 It finds a bigger shell and moves in.
4 shoals
5 to help each other find food; to keep safe
6 They crawl (using tubes on the end of their arms).
7 by winds blowing far out at sea.

Pages 22-25 The magic key

1 Romena
2 Itonga
3 It slipped out of Marcus's hand.
4 a bird
5 The turtle was very wise.
6 I think they would have been very worried and upset because the key belonged to their father and they shouldn't have been touching it. (*or similar*)
7 The golden key was very important because it controlled the tides. The island would be destroyed if the key was lost.
8 She tickled the bird's nose with her pony tail.
9 relieved; happy
10 It was pulled by golden horses.
11 Marcus went red because he knew he had done something naughty that his father didn't know about.
12 It was important.

Pages 26-27 Seaside towns

1 Scarborough, Blackpool or Bude
2 as fishing ports
3 amusement arcades
4 by computers
5 to warn sailors of dangerous rocks
6 The weather is not always fine, so seaside towns need to have things to do inside as well as outside.
7 go to the indoor swimming pool; go to the theatre; or visit the sea life centre
8 there are lots of things to do; they are interesting; they are good places to swim; they have piers and amusement arcades (*or similar*)

Pages 28-29 By the sea

1 It says children laughing in the first verse.
2 Ride on the swings; go on the slide; hook a duck; accept try your luck. *Do not accept activities not mentioned in the poem.*
3 Explore
4 Happy (*or similar*)
5 Accept any two rhyming words, e.g. rides/slides; duck/luck. *Your child may put down some of the close rhymes e.g. laughing/crashing, but in this case direct him or her to the more obvious and clear rhymes.*
6 The weather is sunny; it is fine, it is a sunny day (*or similar*)
7 They are wise; they don't want to be caught; they are hiding from the seagulls.
8 buzzing
9 glide
10 *Accept any answer that refers to an activity mentioned in the poem.*

Marking the practice test

Once you have marked your child's Level 2 practice test, total up the marks from the fiction and non-fiction section. The score will be out of 22 marks.

A child who scores 12-18 on the Level 2 paper is working at about Level 2.

A child who scores 6-12 on the Level 2 paper is working at Level 1.

A child who scores less than 6 is probably working towards Level 1 and would probably do only the reading task in the National Tests.

If your child has got 18 or more correct, let him or her try the Level 3 paper. The score for the Level 3 test will be out of 30 marks. A child who read the Level 3 texts quite easily and scored 20 or more on the Level 3 paper, can be assumed to be working at, or near, Level 3.

Make a note of any areas which your child is finding difficult and give more practice in these areas, or ask your child's teacher for advice.

Regular, short bursts of reading are helpful (10 minutes frequently, is much more effective than 30 minutes once a week). Discussing stories/texts and asking questions helps your child to formulate ideas about books before they need to write them down in a formal setting. Giving children a range of texts to read is also helpful – non-fiction as well as fiction. Your child's school may also be able to suggest some appropriate books at your child's level.